Gardening

Vegetable Gardens

Lori Kinstad Pupeza
ABDO Publishing Company

visit us at
www.abdopub.com

Published by ABDO Publishing Company, 4940 Viking Drive, Edina, Minnesota 55435. Copyright © 2002 by Abdo Consulting Group, Inc. International copyrights reserved in all countries. No part of this book may be reproduced in any form without written permission from the publisher.
Printed in the United States.

Photo credits: Corbis, Corel
Contributing editors: Bob Italia, Tamara L. Britton, Kate A. Furlong, Kristin Van Cleaf
Book design and graphics: Neil Klinepier

Library of Congress Cataloging-in-Publication Data

Pupeza, Lori Kinstad.
    Vegetable Gardens / Lori Kinstad Pupeza.
       p. cm. -- (Gardening)
    Includes index.
    Summary: Describes how to plan and create a vegetable garden, discussing where to plant, what kinds of vegetables to grow, seeds and seedlings, watering, maintenance, and pests.
    ISBN 1-57765-030-1
    1. Vegetable gardening--Juvenile literature. [1. Vegetable gardening. 2. Gardening.] I. Title. II. Series: Pupeza, Lori Kinstad. Gardening.
SB324.P87 1999
635--dc21   98-29329
                                                                                    CIP
                                                                                    AC

Dial Before You Dig
Before digging in your yard with a motorized tiller, call your local utility company to determine the location of underground utility lines.

Contents

Getting Started 4
Where to Plant 6
Making Plans 8
Preparing the Soil 10
Choosing Plants 12
Planting 14
Watering 16
Feeding 18
Garden Care 20
Pests & Helpers 22
A Fun Project 24
In the Fall 26
Planting Tips 28
Glossary 30
Web Sites 31
Index 32

Getting Started

Growing a vegetable garden is a fun and healthy way to grow your own food. Lettuce, carrots, tomatoes, and even strawberries are all easy to grow in a garden.

To start your own garden, choose a location to grow your vegetables. Next, assemble the tools, soil, seeds or **seedlings**, and other gardening supplies you will need. Once you have prepared the soil, it's time to plant your vegetables.

A garden needs care to keep growing. Watering and weeding your garden will ensure tall, healthy plants. There are many different vegetables and fruits to try in your garden. At the end of the summer, you can have a vegetable feast!

Gardening Tools

Turning Soil & Weeding

Hoe

Raking

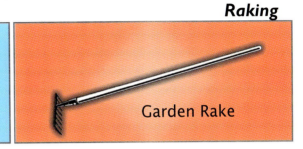

Garden Rake

Watering

Watering Can   Hose

Planting

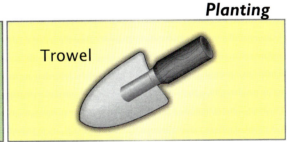

Trowel

Digging

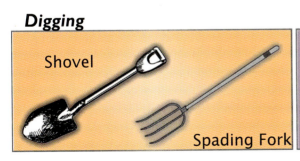

Shovel

Spading Fork

Pest Control

Sprayer

Where to Plant

When planning your garden, choose the best location possible. A good location is an area that gets plenty of sunlight. Vegetables need between six and eight hours of sunlight each day.

If possible, try to plant your garden on a slope. This allows water to drain easily. Try to avoid planting your garden in a low-lying part of your yard. This makes it hard for the water to drain. Plants' stems shouldn't sit in water. It allows mold or **fungus** to grow.

It's also a good idea to plant your garden away from trees and shrubs. If you have too many trees or shrubs near your garden, they will use the water your garden needs. Trees or shrubs may also provide too much shade for your vegetables to grow well.

Choosing a good location is important to the success of your garden.

Making Plans

Now that you have chosen a location, next plan your garden's layout. A good place to start is on paper. Think about what you want your garden to look like. Then draw a map.

Plan for your vegetable rows to run in an east to west direction. Rows that run north to south might shade each other. Plant the tallest vegetables on the north side of the garden.

Remember to leave paths so you can walk through the garden. You will need room to weed between the rows. You will also need space to water the garden and harvest the vegetables.

Now that you have created your garden's layout, take a look at the ground. The next step is to see what sort of soil your garden will have.

Be sure to leave room to walk in your garden.

Preparing the Soil

Once you have your garden plan, it is time to prepare the soil for planting. The area where your garden will be needs to be free of grass and weeds.

Use a shovel or hoe to dig about 8 to 12 inches (20 to 30 cm) into the ground. This turns the earth and makes it softer. Plants' roots need soft soil to grow.

What kind of soil does your garden have? Grab a handful of dirt from your garden. If it crumbles in your hand, you have sandy soil. Add **peat moss**, and the soil will hold more water. If the dirt sticks in a mushy ball, you have clay soil. Add **manure** to clay soil, and the soil will be able to drain water better.

The best soil to have is something in between sandy and clay soil. Try the best you can to **amend** your soil. Your plants will reward you with many vegetables if you plant them in healthy soil.

Determine what type of soil your garden has before you plant.

Choosing Plants

What kinds of fruits or vegetables should you plant in your garden? Pick vegetables that you will enjoy eating. Be sure to choose vegetables that will grow well in your type of soil and climate.

Many vegetables grow well in the hot, summer sun. Watermelons thrive in hot climates, such as the southern United States. Corn also grows well in hot weather, and nothing tastes better than fresh corn on the cob!

Some vegetables also grow well in cooler climates. Carrots grow well in cool weather. They are also fun to yank out of the ground! Lettuce is another vegetable that grows well in cool weather.

A frost map can help you plan when to start your garden. Check your area to see what time of year it is warm enough to plant. Knowing your climate and what time of year to plant will ensure a healthy garden.

Frost Zones

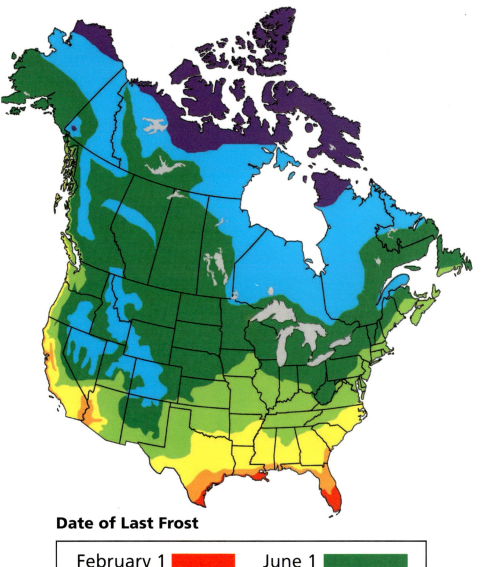

Date of Last Frost

February 1	June 1
March 1	July 1
April 1	August 1
May 1	

Planting

Most vegetables are grown from seeds. Others, like tomatoes and herbs, can be bought as **seedlings** and put directly into the ground.

To plant seeds, use a trowel to make a trench in the soil. Read the seed package to see how far apart the seeds should be, and drop them in. Cover the seeds with soil and mark the row. Water the area each day.

Soon, the seeds will **germinate** into seedlings. The seedlings will grow roots, stems, leaves, and buds. Later the wind, bees, or birds will **pollinate** the flowers. Next, the vegetables and fruits form. When they are done, it is time to harvest.

Seedlings are planted in holes instead of trenches. Gently remove a seedling from its container and place it in the hole. Make sure the base of the stem is even with the ground. Fill the hole with soil and press down around the base of the plant. Water the seedlings immediately.

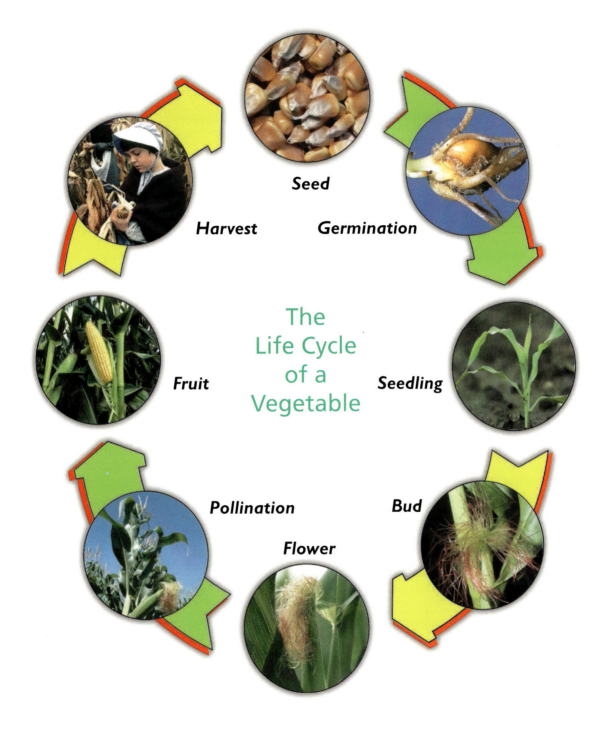

Watering

Watering your garden is important. Many vegetables consist almost entirely of water. Try to water every other day with a sprinkler or hose. During the hottest part of the summer, water your garden every day.

When **seedlings** are small, they don't need much water. Just a small amount each day is enough. Once they grow bigger, leave the sprinkler on or water with a hose for about half an hour at a time.

It is best to water vegetable gardens early in the morning. Morning is the least windy time of day, so the wind won't blow away water intended for the garden.

Watering at night sometimes causes **mildew** or mold to grow on the leaves and stems of vegetables. Mold and mildew will kill your plants.

Watering is an important part of gardening.

Feeding

Plants use **nutrients** from the soil to grow. So, adding compost or **fertilizer** to your garden's soil is important for healthy plants.

Compost is a natural fertilizer. It is made up of **decomposed** grass clippings, leaves, fruit peels, and vegetable scraps.

Many gardeners make their own compost. You can also buy it at a garden center. Mixing compost with your garden's soil is a natural way to add nutrients to your garden.

Chemical fertilizer also adds nutrients to garden soil. Have an adult help you with fertilizer. Read the directions carefully before putting it in your garden. Usually just a little is enough. Fertilizing too much could burn or even kill your plants.

Your plants will grow bigger and faster if you use fertilizer or compost.

Garden Care

Once your garden is planted, it will need regular care in order to grow healthy vegetables and fruits.

Weeding is the biggest task. Weeds take water and **nutrients** from your vegetables. Pull the weeds out at the base. Make sure to get their roots, too. Otherwise, the weeds will grow back.

It is also a good idea to mulch your garden. Mulching means to cover the soil with grass clippings, hay, or wood chips. This helps to smother weeds. Mulch also keeps the top layer of soil from drying out in the sun.

Harvesting fruits and vegetables as soon as they are ready is also important. Harvest as often as you can. Pulling the vegetables off of the plant encourages it to produce more vegetables.

Pests & Helpers

Many animals, such as rabbits and deer, like to eat garden vegetables. The easiest way to keep out bigger animals is to put up a short fence around the garden.

Insects and diseases will also hurt your vegetables. If you see spots on the leaves, pull out the bad plants and throw them away. Pick off any bugs by hand. If you have questions, call a garden center and ask for help from the gardening staff.

Not every animal or insect in your garden is a pest. Toads, worms, bees, butterflies, ladybugs, birds, and bats are helpful to gardens. Birds, bats, ladybugs, and toads all eat harmful insects.

Bees and butterflies **pollinate** plants before the vegetables grow. Worms crawling through the soil make it healthier. Each animal or insect does its own part to help your garden grow.

Rabbits and deer sometimes eat new plants.

Ladybugs and birds will eat harmful insects.

A Fun Project

Making a bean tipi is a fun and easy project. A tipi can be a place to hide for you and your friends. To begin, you will first need three or four tall stakes and some green bean seeds.

To build the tipi, stand the stakes upright to form the frame. Tie the tops of the stakes together with rope. Plant green bean seeds around the base of the stakes. But, don't plant the seeds all the way around. Leave a small opening for a door.

Green beans come in different varieties. Buy the kind that grow into long vines. They are called pole beans. Don't buy bush beans. They will grow short and bushy. You want the vines to grow long enough to spread all over the stakes.

Opposite page: Pole beans have long vines that climb walls and stakes.

In the Fall

When fall comes, harvest all the vegetables you can. After the first freeze, your plants will die. Pull up any **annual** plants, such as tomatoes, and throw them away. Trim back the **perennial** plants, such as strawberries, that will grow again next season.

Once you have harvested and cleared your garden, cover it to protect it. Covering your garden with leaves, compost, or mulch over the winter also helps garden soil get ready for the next spring.

Fall is also a good time to clean your gardening tools. Remove the dirt from your tools to keep them from rusting. Put them someplace dry for the winter, so they will be ready next year.

Opposite page: Harvest all your fruits and vegetables before the first frost.

Planting Tips

When getting started, you will find there are many different vegetables to select. Green beans, carrots, corn, cucumbers, lettuce, peas, squash, and tomatoes are easy to grow.

It's possible to grow more than just vegetables. Try fruit, such as melons, raspberries, or strawberries. Herbs like chives, thyme, sage, basil, rosemary, and mint also grow well in gardens.

The backs of seed packages have helpful tips for choosing vegetables and planting. Most packages include information on what climate and type of soil each plant grows best in, as well as a small frost map.

Many packages also tell how far apart to plant the seeds, and how long they take to **germinate**. And some packages even have suggestions on how to prepare the vegetables once you have harvested them!

front

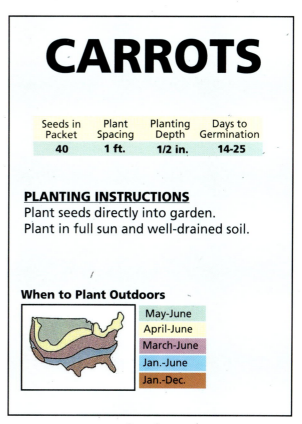

back

The information on seed packages is helpful when choosing plants for your garden.

Glossary

amend - to improve or make better.

annual - a plant that lives for only one growing season.

decompose - to break down into simpler compounds.

fertilizer - a substance used to help plants to grow.

fungus - a group of plants that lack flowers, leaves, and chlorophyll. Mold, mildew, and mushrooms are fungi.

germinate - to sprout and begin to grow.

manure - waste products from animals that can be used as fertilizer.

mildew - mold that rots a plant.

nutrient - something naturally found in soil that helps plants grow.

peat moss - a pale green moss that grows in swamps and bogs.

perennial - a plant that grows every season and dies in the winter.

pollinate - to transfer pollen by wind, birds, or insects from one flower or plant to another.

seedling - a young plant grown from seed but not yet transplanted.

Web Sites

My First Garden
http://www.urbanext.uiuc.edu/firstgarden/
Read about the steps involved in starting a garden at this site from the University of Illinois. Learn how to read the instructions on a seed package, where to plant, what tools to use, and more!

The Great Plant Escape
http://www.urbanext.uiuc.edu/gpe/gpe.html
This site is sponsored by the University of Illinois Extension Services. Young gardeners can help Detective LePlant and his partners Bud and Sprout solve the mystery of the plant life cycle.

These sites are subject to change. Go to your favorite search engine and type in Vegetable Gardens for more sites.

Index

A

animals 14, 22
annual 26

C

climate 12, 14, 28
compost 18, 26

D

drainage 6, 10

F

fertilizer 18
frost map 12, 28

G

germination 14, 28

H

harvest 8, 14, 20, 26, 28

I

insects 14, 22

L

location 4, 6, 8, 10

M

manure 10
mold 6, 16
mulch 20, 26

N

nutrients 18, 20

P

peat moss 10
perennial 26
planning 4, 6, 8, 12, 28
pollination 14, 22

R

roots 10, 14, 20

S

seed packages 14, 28
seedlings 4, 14, 16
seeds 4, 14, 24, 28
shade 6
soil 4, 8, 10, 12, 14, 18, 20, 22, 28
sunlight 6

T

tools 4, 14, 16, 26

W

watering 4, 8, 14, 16
weeding 4, 8, 20